The Travelers
Dream Journal

45 Nights of Traveling on Light

Totukani Amen II

Inner Alchemy's Publishing
Chicago, IL

First Edition

ISBN 978-1-949432-04-6

Any trade names, trademarks, service marks, etc., mentioned in this publication are for identification only. Therefore, any specific company or product mentioned is owned by their respective owner and not by Inner Alchemy's Publishing. Further, the company or product mentioned neither owns, endorses, nor has heard of Inner Alchemy's Publishing. By stating this, we can avoid printing the ®, ™, ©, etc. marks that we might otherwise have to place throughout the text.

The publisher does not participate in, endorse, or have any authority or responsibility concerning private business transactions between our authors and the public.

Published by:

Inner Alchemy's Publishing (Inner Alchemy's)
332 S. Michigan Ave.
Ste 121-C141
Chicago, IL 60604-4434

info@inneralchemys.com
www.inneralchemys.com

Printed in the United States of America

CONTENTS

DISCLAIMER

All information contained within this title is
for entertainment purposes only.

The author or publisher assumes no responsibility
from what one may do with
the information contained herein.

The content of this document should be read or viewed
and utilized as a work of fiction.

Name of Traveler:

_____

Today's Date:

_____

If there is a reason for your travels and you're seeking, rather it is an idea, something tangible or a connection that lies beyond.

And it had to be described in one-word only.

What would you say that one-word is?

_____

Dear Traveler,

I come to you a bit worn as a book that has been by ones side for quite some time, being scuffed and bruised.

There has been a lot going on within the realm as the Draconians have been busy... well so have we.

This is not something to be worried about, as I've been traveling far and wide across the realm, meeting with beings from here and other spaces and conducting a multitude of experiments to prove and, or disprove a thesis.

One such experiment was an atmospheric balloon launch (Project Etheric) which was done twice in the year 2021, once in the country of Illinois (U.S.A.) and another in the country of Georgia (U.S.A.).

We sent up into the upper stratosphere (30 miles above us) equipment to capture a multitude of data, one of which is to see for ourselves the current state of this area of the realm. It was a complete success and contact with other beings from a different space took place which was unexpected but was a pleasant surprise.

Our research is now more important than ever and you traveler, yes you, play an important role in the world to come.

What are the odds that you have acquired this obscure scientifically based dream journal? Ever more so from an esoterically, old world eidetic mind, attempting to give it one last go to see will the sleepers awake? What are the odds? I do very little marketing and when I do advertise it is direct and straight to the point as there is only one-thousand, four-hundred and forty minutes in a day (1440) and I do not have time to waste as there are still many important matters to attend to.

One such matter is will he or she, the 'traveler' repeat yet again the same mistakes, being led down crooked alleyways and swayed off their purpose, their path by vial entities (Draconians) and others who are filled with the pestilence (Muwa)?

Or will the traveler make the difficult choice? The choice to see their path through to the end and by doing this, showing the generations to come what is possible and that true strength lies within not outside one's self. And what gifts were learned and imbued into this soul throughout the journey from beyond space and time that allowed all whose eyes were able to see, and those ears which were able to hear curated thought-forms which transform all from within and ignite what can only be set ablaze with what is ancient, tried and true.

Dreams are much more than random stimuli, impulses and collections of thoughts that one may have while awake which are paraded pass the mouth of those who wish to control.

This dream journal is not a toy, it is a tool.

And as such it was created with purpose.

This purpose shall only be known by me for now, but if you're reading this during a time where I am still here within this realm. Seek out a consultation and, or attend a class.

You will meet other beings on their unique paths all gathering together to share a moment in time, yet again.

Come with pure intent and sincerity.

Your destiny may depend on it.

To your higher self,
Master Amen

SUGGESTIONS FOR MAXIMUM POTENTIAL WHILE TRAVELING

These tips are based on decades of data and observation.

Some of these suggestions may be difficult for some, even if so, suggestions below are for ideal scenarios.

Not in any particular order

- Do not eat 4 hours before bed time

- Do not drink Alcohol

- Do not do pharmaceutical drugs

- Do not do any recreational drugs (DMT, Marijuana, Psilocybin Mushrooms, Peyote, etc.)

- Limit salt intake, seriously really limit this

- Limit sugar intake

- Limit any and all foods, herbs that excite the body/brain, example coffee, ginseng, sugar etc.

- Drink water and only organic/heirloom fresh fruits and/or vegetable juices only, daily

- Drink the best quality water that you're able to acquire

- Do not drink anything at least 1 hour before bedtime

- Do not use computers or be directly in front of electronic devices at least 1 hour before bedtime

- If possible turn-off the electricity to your sleeping room/space entirely via the circuit breaker before bedtime

- No cell phones or computers within your sleeping space at bedtime

- Try to reside in or be in a space with zero artificial E.M.F. (Electro-Magnetic Frequency) bombardment

- Ideally wood floors/tile/stone in your space and not carpet

- Ideally reside or be in a space surrounded by nature, extra bonus points if moving water is nearby (river, lake, stream)

- Fast on a regular basis. At least a few times monthly

- Release any negativity by righting wrongs that you have done. You know what they are, stop ignoring these sub-conscious callings for spiritual correction and correct them with those people. This is probably the most important aspect and certain doors will never open unless you've cleansed your etheric body. And praising strange entities, or trying to invoke extraordinary power that doesn't come from within will not open these doors

There are many more suggestions that can be given to enhance with pin-point accuracy the duration of a dream or the intensity therein.

But for now, if all the above examples were followed one would be ever closer to singularity.

A TOOL FOR DEEPER TRAVELS WITHIN QUANTUM SPACE

LAVENDER DREAMS OF A BLUE LOTUS

Greetings Travelers,

Reaching out to you through space and time, with a new tool to help you on your journey.

Many of you know of my research as some of you have been part of it.

I recently was Looking through over 20 years of data and came upon an interesting observation.

When the bridge is connected between our world and the next, when many of you are out yonder speaking to those in other spaces digging deeper within twilight to bring back those premonitions, wise words and tools that can be used within our space and time.

Many of you have complained that there are breaks in the transmission, and between these gaps pertinent information is shared but it is forever lost as when you rejoin, the conversation is well pass the initial point.

For you, traveler... my late nights were not wasted as only thing the neighbors heard was eureka! As I perfected a serum that I imbued within the form of a salve.

This tool, this salve, I call 'Lavender Dreams of a Blue Lotus'

Before your travels, rub a dime sized amount at the bottom of each foot, and make sure you rub it in as much as possible. Each night it is used the greater effect shall be had.

Your travels shall be more vivid, and transmission breaks will no longer occur.

I look forward to what you bring back.

Available at: www.metacenterchicago.com

DREAMSCAPE
An Ancient Herbal Blend

May Induce Vivid and Prophetic Dreams

Made with only Organic and/or Wild Crafted Ingredients.

Traditionally used as an incense or smudge

Disclaimer

- Do not use if pregnant

- Do not use if nursing

- Do not use if operating a motor vehicle

- Do not use if suffering from any physical or mental health ailment

Available at: www.metacenterchicago.com

INSTRUCTIONS OF USE:

TERM	MEANING
DATE	Date that sleep occurred – Write down before bedtime –
BED TIME	Time that you went to sleep
AWAKENED TIME	Time that you awoke
SLEEP DURATION	How long were you asleep
TOSS & TURNED	Did you move around a lot during the night
COLD	Were you cold during the night
HOT	Were you hot during the night
CATEGORY	The general overall theme of your dream – What did it deal with –
ATTRIBUTES	Various attributes that were present within the dream that can give insight when analyzed
CHARACTERS	Were any specific characters within your dream or were you alone
EMOTIONS	Emotonal state during your travels
JOURNAL	Describe in detail what took place during your travels
SPECIAL NOTES	Did anything take place that should be noted and/or is of great importance

Date: _____

Bed Time: _____   Toss & Turned: ☐ yes ☐ no

Awakened Time: _____   Cold: ☐ yes ☐ no

Sleep Duration: _____   Hot: ☐ yes ☐ no

CATEGORY

☐ Premonition   ☐ Ancestral   ☐ Subconscious   ☐ Employment

☐ Current/Past Event   ☐ Abuse   ☐ Trauma   ☐ Nudity

☐ Sexual   ☐ Family   ☐ Not Sure

Something Else: _____

ATTRIBUTES

☐ Colorful   ☐ Black & White   ☐ Loud/Noisy   ☐ Quiet   ☐ Sunny

☐ Dark   ☐ Water   ☐ Earth/Dirt   ☐ Fire   ☐ Sky

☐ Wind/Tornado   ☐ Cold   ☐ Hot   ☐ Wet   ☐ Not Sure

Something Else: _____

CHARACTERS

☐ People   ☐ Animals   ☐ Spirits

☐ Angels   ☐ Demons   ☐ Gods

☐ Not Sure   ☐ None   Something Else: _____

EMOTIONS

☐ Anger   ☐ Love   ☐ Guilt   ☐ Sadness

☐ Jealousy   ☐ Confusion   ☐ Grief   ☐ Happiness

☐ Fear   ☐ Shock   ☐ Courage   ☐ Not Sure

Something Else: _____

JOURNAL

_____
_____
_____
_____
_____
_____
_____
_____
_____
_____
_____
_____
_____
_____
_____
_____
_____
_____
_____
_____
_____
_____
_____
_____
_____

SPECIAL NOTES

_____
_____
_____
_____

Date: _____

Bed Time: _____   Toss & Turned: ☐ yes ☐ no
Awakened Time: _____   Cold: ☐ yes ☐ no
Sleep Duration: _____   Hot: ☐ yes ☐ no

CATEGORY

☐ Premonition   ☐ Ancestral   ☐ Subconscious   ☐ Employment
☐ Current/Past Event   ☐ Abuse   ☐ Trauma   ☐ Nudity
☐ Sexual   ☐ Family   ☐ Not Sure

Something Else: _____

ATTRIBUTES

☐ Colorful   ☐ Black & White   ☐ Loud/Noisy   ☐ Quiet   ☐ Sunny
☐ Dark   ☐ Water   ☐ Earth/Dirt   ☐ Fire   ☐ Sky
☐ Wind/Tornado   ☐ Cold   ☐ Hot   ☐ Wet   ☐ Not Sure

Something Else: _____

CHARACTERS

☐ People   ☐ Animals   ☐ Spirits
☐ Angels   ☐ Demons   ☐ Gods
☐ Not Sure   ☐ None   Something Else: _____

EMOTIONS

☐ Anger   ☐ Love   ☐ Guilt   ☐ Sadness
☐ Jealousy   ☐ Confusion   ☐ Grief   ☐ Happiness
☐ Fear   ☐ Shock   ☐ Courage   ☐ Not Sure

Something Else: _____

JOURNAL

(blank lined page)

SPECIAL NOTES

Date: _____

Bed Time: _____

Awakened Time: _____

Sleep Duration: _____

Toss & Turned: ☐ yes ☐ no

Cold: ☐ yes ☐ no

Hot: ☐ yes ☐ no

CATEGORY

☐ Premonition   ☐ Ancestral   ☐ Subconscious   ☐ Employment

☐ Current/Past Event   ☐ Abuse   ☐ Trauma   ☐ Nudity

☐ Sexual   ☐ Family   ☐ Not Sure

Something Else: _____

ATTRIBUTES

☐ Colorful   ☐ Black & White   ☐ Loud/Noisy   ☐ Quiet   ☐ Sunny

☐ Dark   ☐ Water   ☐ Earth/Dirt   ☐ Fire   ☐ Sky

☐ Wind/Tornado   ☐ Cold   ☐ Hot   ☐ Wet   ☐ Not Sure

Something Else: _____

CHARACTERS

☐ People   ☐ Animals   ☐ Spirits

☐ Angels   ☐ Demons   ☐ Gods

☐ Not Sure   ☐ None   Something Else: _____

EMOTIONS

☐ Anger   ☐ Love   ☐ Guilt   ☐ Sadness

☐ Jealousy   ☐ Confusion   ☐ Grief   ☐ Happiness

☐ Fear   ☐ Shock   ☐ Courage   ☐ Not Sure

Something Else: _____

JOURNAL

_____
_____
_____
_____
_____
_____
_____
_____
_____
_____
_____
_____
_____
_____
_____
_____
_____
_____
_____
_____
_____
_____

SPECIAL NOTES

_____
_____
_____
_____

Date: _____

Bed Time: _____

Awakened Time: _____

Sleep Duration: _____

Toss & Turned: ☐ yes ☐ no

Cold: ☐ yes ☐ no

Hot: ☐ yes ☐ no

CATEGORY

☐ Premonition ☐ Ancestral ☐ Subconscious ☐ Employment

☐ Current/Past Event ☐ Abuse ☐ Trauma ☐ Nudity

☐ Sexual ☐ Family ☐ Not Sure

Something Else: _____

ATTRIBUTES

☐ Colorful ☐ Black & White ☐ Loud/Noisy ☐ Quiet ☐ Sunny

☐ Dark ☐ Water ☐ Earth/Dirt ☐ Fire ☐ Sky

☐ Wind/Tornado ☐ Cold ☐ Hot ☐ Wet ☐ Not Sure

Something Else: _____

CHARACTERS

☐ People ☐ Animals ☐ Spirits

☐ Angels ☐ Demons ☐ Gods

☐ Not Sure ☐ None

Something Else: _____

EMOTIONS

☐ Anger ☐ Love ☐ Guilt ☐ Sadness

☐ Jealousy ☐ Confusion ☐ Grief ☐ Happiness

☐ Fear ☐ Shock ☐ Courage ☐ Not Sure

Something Else: _____

JOURNAL

_____
_____
_____
_____
_____
_____
_____
_____
_____
_____
_____
_____
_____
_____
_____
_____
_____
_____
_____
_____
_____
_____
_____
_____
_____

SPECIAL NOTES

_____
_____
_____
_____

Date: _____

Bed Time: _____　　　Toss & Turned: ☐ yes ☐ no
Awakened Time: _____　　　Cold: ☐ yes ☐ no
Sleep Duration: _____　　　Hot: ☐ yes ☐ no

CATEGORY

☐ Premonition　　☐ Ancestral　　☐ Subconscious　　☐ Employment
☐ Current/Past Event　　☐ Abuse　　☐ Trauma　　☐ Nudity
☐ Sexual　　☐ Family　　☐ Not Sure

Something Else: _____

ATTRIBUTES

☐ Colorful　　☐ Black & White　　☐ Loud/Noisy　　☐ Quiet　　☐ Sunny
☐ Dark　　☐ Water　　☐ Earth/Dirt　　☐ Fire　　☐ Sky
☐ Wind/Tornado　　☐ Cold　　☐ Hot　　☐ Wet　　☐ Not Sure

Something Else: _____

CHARACTERS

☐ People　　☐ Animals　　☐ Spirits
☐ Angels　　☐ Demons　　☐ Gods
☐ Not Sure　　☐ None　　Something Else: _____

EMOTIONS

☐ Anger　　☐ Love　　☐ Guilt　　☐ Sadness
☐ Jealousy　　☐ Confusion　　☐ Grief　　☐ Happiness
☐ Fear　　☐ Shock　　☐ Courage　　☐ Not Sure

Something Else: _____

JOURNAL

_____
_____
_____
_____
_____
_____
_____
_____
_____
_____
_____
_____
_____
_____
_____
_____
_____
_____
_____
_____
_____
_____
_____

SPECIAL NOTES

_____
_____
_____
_____

Date: _____

Bed Time: _____   Toss & Turned: ☐ yes ☐ no

Awakened Time: _____   Cold: ☐ yes ☐ no

Sleep Duration: _____   Hot: ☐ yes ☐ no

CATEGORY

☐ Premonition   ☐ Ancestral   ☐ Subconscious   ☐ Employment

☐ Current/Past Event   ☐ Abuse   ☐ Trauma   ☐ Nudity

☐ Sexual   ☐ Family   ☐ Not Sure

Something Else: _____

ATTRIBUTES

☐ Colorful   ☐ Black & White   ☐ Loud/Noisy   ☐ Quiet   ☐ Sunny

☐ Dark   ☐ Water   ☐ Earth/Dirt   ☐ Fire   ☐ Sky

☐ Wind/Tornado   ☐ Cold   ☐ Hot   ☐ Wet   ☐ Not Sure

Something Else: _____

CHARACTERS

☐ People   ☐ Animals   ☐ Spirits

☐ Angels   ☐ Demons   ☐ Gods

☐ Not Sure   ☐ None   Something Else: _____

EMOTIONS

☐ Anger   ☐ Love   ☐ Guilt   ☐ Sadness

☐ Jealousy   ☐ Confusion   ☐ Grief   ☐ Happiness

☐ Fear   ☐ Shock   ☐ Courage   ☐ Not Sure

Something Else: _____

_____
_____
_____
_____
_____
_____
_____
_____
_____
_____
_____
_____
_____
_____
_____
_____
_____
_____
_____
_____
_____
_____
_____

SPECIAL NOTES

_____
_____
_____
_____

Date: _____

Bed Time: _____

Awakened Time: _____

Sleep Duration: _____

Toss & Turned: ☐ yes ☐ no

Cold: ☐ yes ☐ no

Hot: ☐ yes ☐ no

CATEGORY

☐ Premonition ☐ Ancestral ☐ Subconscious ☐ Employment

☐ Current/Past Event ☐ Abuse ☐ Trauma ☐ Nudity

☐ Sexual ☐ Family ☐ Not Sure

Something Else: _____

ATTRIBUTES

☐ Colorful ☐ Black & White ☐ Loud/Noisy ☐ Quiet ☐ Sunny

☐ Dark ☐ Water ☐ Earth/Dirt ☐ Fire ☐ Sky

☐ Wind/Tornado ☐ Cold ☐ Hot ☐ Wet ☐ Not Sure

Something Else: _____

CHARACTERS

☐ People ☐ Animals ☐ Spirits

☐ Angels ☐ Demons ☐ Gods

☐ Not Sure ☐ None Something Else: _____

EMOTIONS

☐ Anger ☐ Love ☐ Guilt ☐ Sadness

☐ Jealousy ☐ Confusion ☐ Grief ☐ Happiness

☐ Fear ☐ Shock ☐ Courage ☐ Not Sure

Something Else: _____

JOURNAL

_____
_____
_____
_____
_____
_____
_____
_____
_____
_____
_____
_____
_____
_____
_____
_____
_____
_____
_____
_____
_____
_____
_____
_____

SPECIAL NOTES

_____
_____
_____
_____

Date: _____

Bed Time: _____
Awakened Time: _____
Sleep Duration: _____

Toss & Turned: ☐ yes ☐ no
Cold: ☐ yes ☐ no
Hot: ☐ yes ☐ no

CATEGORY

☐ Premonition
☐ Current/Past Event
☐ Sexual

☐ Ancestral
☐ Abuse
☐ Family

☐ Subconscious
☐ Trauma
☐ Not Sure

☐ Employment
☐ Nudity

Something Else: _____

ATTRIBUTES

☐ Colorful
☐ Dark
☐ Wind/Tornado

☐ Black & White
☐ Water
☐ Cold

☐ Loud/Noisy
☐ Earth/Dirt
☐ Hot

☐ Quiet
☐ Fire
☐ Wet

☐ Sunny
☐ Sky
☐ Not Sure

Something Else: _____

CHARACTERS

☐ People
☐ Angels
☐ Not Sure

☐ Animals
☐ Demons
☐ None

☐ Spirits
☐ Gods

Something Else: _____

EMOTIONS

☐ Anger
☐ Jealousy
☐ Fear

☐ Love
☐ Confusion
☐ Shock

☐ Guilt
☐ Grief
☐ Courage

☐ Sadness
☐ Happiness
☐ Not Sure

Something Else: _____

JOURNAL

_____
_____
_____
_____
_____
_____
_____
_____
_____
_____
_____
_____
_____
_____
_____
_____
_____
_____
_____
_____
_____
_____
_____
_____

SPECIAL NOTES

_____
_____
_____
_____

Date: _____

Bed Time: _____

Awakened Time: _____

Sleep Duration: _____

Toss & Turned: ☐ yes ☐ no

Cold: ☐ yes ☐ no

Hot: ☐ yes ☐ no

CATEGORY

☐ Premonition   ☐ Ancestral   ☐ Subconscious   ☐ Employment

☐ Current/Past Event   ☐ Abuse   ☐ Trauma   ☐ Nudity

☐ Sexual   ☐ Family   ☐ Not Sure

Something Else: _____

ATTRIBUTES

☐ Colorful   ☐ Black & White   ☐ Loud/Noisy   ☐ Quiet   ☐ Sunny

☐ Dark   ☐ Water   ☐ Earth/Dirt   ☐ Fire   ☐ Sky

☐ Wind/Tornado   ☐ Cold   ☐ Hot   ☐ Wet   ☐ Not Sure

Something Else: _____

CHARACTERS

☐ People   ☐ Animals   ☐ Spirits

☐ Angels   ☐ Demons   ☐ Gods

☐ Not Sure   ☐ None   Something Else: _____

EMOTIONS

☐ Anger   ☐ Love   ☐ Guilt   ☐ Sadness

☐ Jealousy   ☐ Confusion   ☐ Grief   ☐ Happiness

☐ Fear   ☐ Shock   ☐ Courage   ☐ Not Sure

Something Else: _____

JOURNAL

_____
_____
_____
_____
_____
_____
_____
_____
_____
_____
_____
_____
_____
_____
_____
_____
_____
_____
_____
_____
_____
_____
_____
_____

SPECIAL NOTES

_____
_____
_____
_____

Date: _____

Bed Time: _____   Toss & Turned: ☐ yes ☐ no
Awakened Time: _____   Cold: ☐ yes ☐ no
Sleep Duration: _____   Hot: ☐ yes ☐ no

CATEGORY

☐ Premonition   ☐ Ancestral   ☐ Subconscious   ☐ Employment
☐ Current/Past Event ☐ Abuse   ☐ Trauma   ☐ Nudity
☐ Sexual   ☐ Family   ☐ Not Sure

Something Else: _____

ATTRIBUTES

☐ Colorful   ☐ Black & White   ☐ Loud/Noisy   ☐ Quiet   ☐ Sunny
☐ Dark   ☐ Water   ☐ Earth/Dirt   ☐ Fire   ☐ Sky
☐ Wind/Tornado   ☐ Cold   ☐ Hot   ☐ Wet   ☐ Not Sure

Something Else: _____

CHARACTERS

☐ People   ☐ Animals   ☐ Spirits
☐ Angels   ☐ Demons   ☐ Gods
☐ Not Sure   ☐ None   Something Else: _____

EMOTIONS

☐ Anger   ☐ Love   ☐ Guilt   ☐ Sadness
☐ Jealousy   ☐ Confusion   ☐ Grief   ☐ Happiness
☐ Fear   ☐ Shock   ☐ Courage   ☐ Not Sure

Something Else: _____

- 34 -

JOURNAL

_____

SPECIAL NOTES

_____

Date: _____

Bed Time: _____
Awakened Time: _____
Sleep Duration: _____

Toss & Turned: ☐ yes ☐ no
Cold: ☐ yes ☐ no
Hot: ☐ yes ☐ no

CATEGORY

☐ Premonition
☐ Current/Past Event
☐ Sexual

☐ Ancestral
☐ Abuse
☐ Family

☐ Subconscious
☐ Trauma
☐ Not Sure

☐ Employment
☐ Nudity

Something Else: _____

ATTRIBUTES

☐ Colorful
☐ Dark
☐ Wind/Tornado

☐ Black & White
☐ Water
☐ Cold

☐ Loud/Noisy
☐ Earth/Dirt
☐ Hot

☐ Quiet
☐ Fire
☐ Wet

☐ Sunny
☐ Sky
☐ Not Sure

Something Else: _____

CHARACTERS

☐ People
☐ Angels
☐ Not Sure

☐ Animals
☐ Demons
☐ None

☐ Spirits
☐ Gods

Something Else: _____

EMOTIONS

☐ Anger
☐ Jealousy
☐ Fear

☐ Love
☐ Confusion
☐ Shock

☐ Guilt
☐ Grief
☐ Courage

☐ Sadness
☐ Happiness
☐ Not Sure

Something Else: _____

JOURNAL

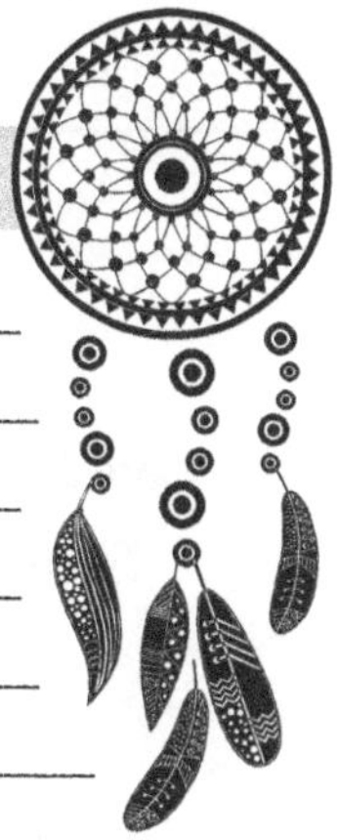

_____
_____
_____
_____
_____
_____
_____
_____
_____
_____
_____
_____
_____
_____
_____
_____
_____
_____
_____
_____
_____
_____
_____
_____
_____

SPECIAL NOTES

_____
_____
_____
_____

Date: _____

Bed Time: _____   Toss & Turned: ☐ yes ☐ no

Awakened Time: _____   Cold: ☐ yes ☐ no

Sleep Duration: _____   Hot: ☐ yes ☐ no

CATEGORY

☐ Premonition   ☐ Ancestral   ☐ Subconscious   ☐ Employment

☐ Current/Past Event   ☐ Abuse   ☐ Trauma   ☐ Nudity

☐ Sexual   ☐ Family   ☐ Not Sure

Something Else: _____

ATTRIBUTES

☐ Colorful   ☐ Black & White   ☐ Loud/Noisy   ☐ Quiet   ☐ Sunny

☐ Dark   ☐ Water   ☐ Earth/Dirt   ☐ Fire   ☐ Sky

☐ Wind/Tornado   ☐ Cold   ☐ Hot   ☐ Wet   ☐ Not Sure

Something Else: _____

CHARACTERS

☐ People   ☐ Animals   ☐ Spirits

☐ Angels   ☐ Demons   ☐ Gods

☐ Not Sure   ☐ None   Something Else: _____

EMOTIONS

☐ Anger   ☐ Love   ☐ Guilt   ☐ Sadness

☐ Jealousy   ☐ Confusion   ☐ Grief   ☐ Happiness

☐ Fear   ☐ Shock   ☐ Courage   ☐ Not Sure

Something Else: _____

JOURNAL

_____
_____
_____
_____
_____
_____
_____
_____
_____
_____
_____
_____
_____
_____
_____
_____
_____
_____
_____
_____
_____
_____
_____

SPECIAL NOTES

_____
_____
_____
_____

Date: _____

Bed Time: _____
Awakened Time: _____
Sleep Duration: _____

Toss & Turned: ☐ yes ☐ no
Cold: ☐ yes ☐ no
Hot: ☐ yes ☐ no

CATEGORY

☐ Premonition ☐ Ancestral ☐ Subconscious ☐ Employment
☐ Current/Past Event ☐ Abuse ☐ Trauma ☐ Nudity
☐ Sexual ☐ Family ☐ Not Sure

Something Else: _____

ATTRIBUTES

☐ Colorful ☐ Black & White ☐ Loud/Noisy ☐ Quiet ☐ Sunny
☐ Dark ☐ Water ☐ Earth/Dirt ☐ Fire ☐ Sky
☐ Wind/Tornado ☐ Cold ☐ Hot ☐ Wet ☐ Not Sure

Something Else: _____

CHARACTERS

☐ People ☐ Animals ☐ Spirits
☐ Angels ☐ Demons ☐ Gods
☐ Not Sure ☐ None

Something Else: _____

EMOTIONS

☐ Anger ☐ Love ☐ Guilt ☐ Sadness
☐ Jealousy ☐ Confusion ☐ Grief ☐ Happiness
☐ Fear ☐ Shock ☐ Courage ☐ Not Sure

Something Else: _____

JOURNAL

_____
_____
_____
_____
_____
_____
_____
_____
_____
_____
_____
_____
_____
_____
_____
_____
_____
_____
_____
_____
_____
_____
_____
_____

SPECIAL NOTES

_____
_____
_____
_____

Date: _____

Bed Time: _____ Toss & Turned: ☐ yes ☐ no
Awakened Time: _____ Cold: ☐ yes ☐ no
Sleep Duration: _____ Hot: ☐ yes ☐ no

CATEGORY

☐ Premonition   ☐ Ancestral   ☐ Subconscious   ☐ Employment
☐ Current/Past Event   ☐ Abuse   ☐ Trauma   ☐ Nudity
☐ Sexual   ☐ Family   ☐ Not Sure

Something Else: _____

ATTRIBUTES

☐ Colorful   ☐ Black & White   ☐ Loud/Noisy   ☐ Quiet   ☐ Sunny
☐ Dark   ☐ Water   ☐ Earth/Dirt   ☐ Fire   ☐ Sky
☐ Wind/Tornado   ☐ Cold   ☐ Hot   ☐ Wet   ☐ Not Sure

Something Else: _____

CHARACTERS

☐ People   ☐ Animals   ☐ Spirits
☐ Angels   ☐ Demons   ☐ Gods
☐ Not Sure   ☐ None   Something Else: _____

EMOTIONS

☐ Anger   ☐ Love   ☐ Guilt   ☐ Sadness
☐ Jealousy   ☐ Confusion   ☐ Grief   ☐ Happiness
☐ Fear   ☐ Shock   ☐ Courage   ☐ Not Sure

Something Else: _____

JOURNAL

SPECIAL NOTES

Date: _____

Bed Time: _____   Toss & Turned: ☐ yes ☐ no
Awakened Time: _____   Cold: ☐ yes ☐ no
Sleep Duration: _____   Hot: ☐ yes ☐ no

CATEGORY

☐ Premonition   ☐ Ancestral   ☐ Subconscious   ☐ Employment
☐ Current/Past Event   ☐ Abuse   ☐ Trauma   ☐ Nudity
☐ Sexual   ☐ Family   ☐ Not Sure

Something Else: _____

ATTRIBUTES

☐ Colorful   ☐ Black & White   ☐ Loud/Noisy   ☐ Quiet   ☐ Sunny
☐ Dark   ☐ Water   ☐ Earth/Dirt   ☐ Fire   ☐ Sky
☐ Wind/Tornado   ☐ Cold   ☐ Hot   ☐ Wet   ☐ Not Sure

Something Else: _____

CHARACTERS

☐ People   ☐ Animals   ☐ Spirits
☐ Angels   ☐ Demons   ☐ Gods
☐ Not Sure   ☐ None   Something Else: _____

EMOTIONS

☐ Anger   ☐ Love   ☐ Guilt   ☐ Sadness
☐ Jealousy   ☐ Confusion   ☐ Grief   ☐ Happiness
☐ Fear   ☐ Shock   ☐ Courage   ☐ Not Sure

Something Else: _____

_____
_____
_____
_____
_____
_____
_____
_____
_____
_____
_____
_____
_____
_____
_____
_____
_____
_____
_____
_____
_____
_____
_____
_____
_____

SPECIAL NOTES

_____
_____
_____
_____

Date: _____

Bed Time: _____   Toss & Turned: ☐ yes ☐ no
Awakened Time: _____   Cold: ☐ yes ☐ no
Sleep Duration: _____   Hot: ☐ yes ☐ no

CATEGORY

☐ Premonition   ☐ Ancestral   ☐ Subconscious   ☐ Employment
☐ Current/Past Event ☐ Abuse   ☐ Trauma   ☐ Nudity
☐ Sexual   ☐ Family   ☐ Not Sure

Something Else: _____

ATTRIBUTES

☐ Colorful   ☐ Black & White   ☐ Loud/Noisy   ☐ Quiet   ☐ Sunny
☐ Dark   ☐ Water   ☐ Earth/Dirt   ☐ Fire   ☐ Sky
☐ Wind/Tornado   ☐ Cold   ☐ Hot   ☐ Wet   ☐ Not Sure

Something Else: _____

CHARACTERS

☐ People   ☐ Animals   ☐ Spirits
☐ Angels   ☐ Demons   ☐ Gods
☐ Not Sure   ☐ None

Something Else: _____

EMOTIONS

☐ Anger   ☐ Love   ☐ Guilt   ☐ Sadness
☐ Jealousy   ☐ Confusion   ☐ Grief   ☐ Happiness
☐ Fear   ☐ Shock   ☐ Courage   ☐ Not Sure

Something Else: _____

JOURNAL

_____
_____
_____
_____
_____
_____
_____
_____
_____
_____
_____
_____
_____
_____
_____
_____
_____
_____
_____
_____
_____
_____
_____

SPECIAL NOTES

_____
_____
_____
_____

Date: _____

Bed Time: _____   Toss & Turned: ☐ yes ☐ no

Awakened Time: _____   Cold: ☐ yes ☐ no

Sleep Duration: _____   Hot: ☐ yes ☐ no

CATEGORY

☐ Premonition   ☐ Ancestral   ☐ Subconscious   ☐ Employment

☐ Current/Past Event   ☐ Abuse   ☐ Trauma   ☐ Nudity

☐ Sexual   ☐ Family   ☐ Not Sure

Something Else: _____

ATTRIBUTES

☐ Colorful   ☐ Black & White   ☐ Loud/Noisy   ☐ Quiet   ☐ Sunny

☐ Dark   ☐ Water   ☐ Earth/Dirt   ☐ Fire   ☐ Sky

☐ Wind/Tornado   ☐ Cold   ☐ Hot   ☐ Wet   ☐ Not Sure

Something Else: _____

CHARACTERS

☐ People   ☐ Animals   ☐ Spirits

☐ Angels   ☐ Demons   ☐ Gods

☐ Not Sure   ☐ None   Something Else: _____

EMOTIONS

☐ Anger   ☐ Love   ☐ Guilt   ☐ Sadness

☐ Jealousy   ☐ Confusion   ☐ Grief   ☐ Happiness

☐ Fear   ☐ Shock   ☐ Courage   ☐ Not Sure

Something Else: _____

JOURNAL

_____
_____
_____
_____
_____
_____
_____
_____
_____
_____
_____
_____
_____
_____
_____
_____
_____
_____
_____
_____
_____
_____
_____

SPECIAL NOTES

_____
_____
_____
_____

Date: _____

Bed Time: _____
Awakened Time: _____
Sleep Duration: _____

Toss & Turned: ☐ yes ☐ no
Cold: ☐ yes ☐ no
Hot: ☐ yes ☐ no

CATEGORY

☐ Premonition ☐ Ancestral ☐ Subconscious ☐ Employment
☐ Current/Past Event ☐ Abuse ☐ Trauma ☐ Nudity
☐ Sexual ☐ Family ☐ Not Sure

Something Else: _____

ATTRIBUTES

☐ Colorful ☐ Black & White ☐ Loud/Noisy ☐ Quiet ☐ Sunny
☐ Dark ☐ Water ☐ Earth/Dirt ☐ Fire ☐ Sky
☐ Wind/Tornado ☐ Cold ☐ Hot ☐ Wet ☐ Not Sure

Something Else: _____

CHARACTERS

☐ People ☐ Animals ☐ Spirits
☐ Angels ☐ Demons ☐ Gods
☐ Not Sure ☐ None

Something Else: _____

EMOTIONS

☐ Anger ☐ Love ☐ Guilt ☐ Sadness
☐ Jealousy ☐ Confusion ☐ Grief ☐ Happiness
☐ Fear ☐ Shock ☐ Courage ☐ Not Sure

Something Else: _____

JOURNAL

_____
_____
_____
_____
_____
_____
_____
_____
_____
_____
_____
_____
_____
_____
_____
_____
_____
_____
_____
_____
_____
_____
_____

SPECIAL NOTES

_____
_____
_____
_____

Date: _____

Bed Time: _____
Awakened Time: _____
Sleep Duration: _____

Toss & Turned: ☐ yes ☐ no
Cold: ☐ yes ☐ no
Hot: ☐ yes ☐ no

CATEGORY

☐ Premonition
☐ Current/Past Event
☐ Sexual

☐ Ancestral
☐ Abuse
☐ Family

☐ Subconscious
☐ Trauma
☐ Not Sure

☐ Employment
☐ Nudity

Something Else: _____

ATTRIBUTES

☐ Colorful
☐ Dark
☐ Wind/Tornado

☐ Black & White
☐ Water
☐ Cold

☐ Loud/Noisy
☐ Earth/Dirt
☐ Hot

☐ Quiet
☐ Fire
☐ Wet

☐ Sunny
☐ Sky
☐ Not Sure

Something Else: _____

CHARACTERS

☐ People
☐ Angels
☐ Not Sure

☐ Animals
☐ Demons
☐ None

☐ Spirits
☐ Gods

Something Else: _____

EMOTIONS

☐ Anger
☐ Jealousy
☐ Fear

☐ Love
☐ Confusion
☐ Shock

☐ Guilt
☐ Grief
☐ Courage

☐ Sadness
☐ Happiness
☐ Not Sure

Something Else: _____

_____
_____
_____
_____
_____
_____
_____
_____
_____
_____
_____
_____
_____
_____
_____
_____
_____
_____
_____
_____
_____
_____
_____
_____

SPECIAL NOTES

_____
_____
_____
_____

_____ _____

Date: _____

Bed Time: _____

Awakened Time: _____

Sleep Duration: _____

Toss & Turned: ☐ yes ☐ no

Cold: ☐ yes ☐ no

Hot: ☐ yes ☐ no

CATEGORY

☐ Premonition   ☐ Ancestral   ☐ Subconscious   ☐ Employment

☐ Current/Past Event   ☐ Abuse   ☐ Trauma   ☐ Nudity

☐ Sexual   ☐ Family   ☐ Not Sure

Something Else: _____

ATTRIBUTES

☐ Colorful   ☐ Black & White   ☐ Loud/Noisy   ☐ Quiet   ☐ Sunny

☐ Dark   ☐ Water   ☐ Earth/Dirt   ☐ Fire   ☐ Sky

☐ Wind/Tornado   ☐ Cold   ☐ Hot   ☐ Wet   ☐ Not Sure

Something Else: _____

CHARACTERS

☐ People   ☐ Animals   ☐ Spirits

☐ Angels   ☐ Demons   ☐ Gods

☐ Not Sure   ☐ None   Something Else: _____

EMOTIONS

☐ Anger   ☐ Love   ☐ Guilt   ☐ Sadness

☐ Jealousy   ☐ Confusion   ☐ Grief   ☐ Happiness

☐ Fear   ☐ Shock   ☐ Courage   ☐ Not Sure

Something Else: _____

_____
_____
_____
_____
_____
_____
_____
_____
_____
_____
_____
_____
_____
_____
_____
_____
_____
_____
_____
_____
_____
_____

SPECIAL NOTES

_____
_____
_____
_____

Date: _____

Bed Time: _____   Toss & Turned: ☐ yes ☐ no

Awakened Time: _____   Cold: ☐ yes ☐ no

Sleep Duration: _____   Hot: ☐ yes ☐ no

CATEGORY

☐ Premonition   ☐ Ancestral   ☐ Subconscious   ☐ Employment

☐ Current/Past Event   ☐ Abuse   ☐ Trauma   ☐ Nudity

☐ Sexual   ☐ Family   ☐ Not Sure

Something Else: _____

ATTRIBUTES

☐ Colorful   ☐ Black & White   ☐ Loud/Noisy   ☐ Quiet   ☐ Sunny

☐ Dark   ☐ Water   ☐ Earth/Dirt   ☐ Fire   ☐ Sky

☐ Wind/Tornado   ☐ Cold   ☐ Hot   ☐ Wet   ☐ Not Sure

Something Else: _____

CHARACTERS

☐ People   ☐ Animals   ☐ Spirits

☐ Angels   ☐ Demons   ☐ Gods

☐ Not Sure   ☐ None   Something Else: _____

EMOTIONS

☐ Anger   ☐ Love   ☐ Guilt   ☐ Sadness

☐ Jealousy   ☐ Confusion   ☐ Grief   ☐ Happiness

☐ Fear   ☐ Shock   ☐ Courage   ☐ Not Sure

Something Else: _____

JOURNAL

SPECIAL NOTES

Date: _____

Bed Time: _____

Awakened Time: _____

Sleep Duration: _____

Toss & Turned: ☐ yes ☐ no

Cold: ☐ yes ☐ no

Hot: ☐ yes ☐ no

CATEGORY

☐ Premonition ☐ Ancestral ☐ Subconscious ☐ Employment

☐ Current/Past Event ☐ Abuse ☐ Trauma ☐ Nudity

☐ Sexual ☐ Family ☐ Not Sure

Something Else: _____

ATTRIBUTES

☐ Colorful ☐ Black & White ☐ Loud/Noisy ☐ Quiet ☐ Sunny

☐ Dark ☐ Water ☐ Earth/Dirt ☐ Fire ☐ Sky

☐ Wind/Tornado ☐ Cold ☐ Hot ☐ Wet ☐ Not Sure

Something Else: _____

CHARACTERS

☐ People ☐ Animals ☐ Spirits

☐ Angels ☐ Demons ☐ Gods

☐ Not Sure ☐ None Something Else: _____

EMOTIONS

☐ Anger ☐ Love ☐ Guilt ☐ Sadness

☐ Jealousy ☐ Confusion ☐ Grief ☐ Happiness

☐ Fear ☐ Shock ☐ Courage ☐ Not Sure

Something Else: _____

JOURNAL

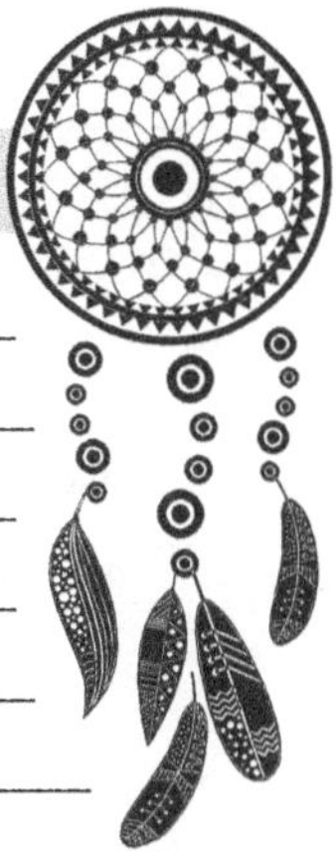

_____
_____
_____
_____
_____
_____
_____
_____
_____
_____
_____
_____
_____
_____
_____
_____
_____
_____
_____
_____
_____
_____
_____

SPECIAL NOTES

_____
_____
_____
_____

Date: _____

Bed Time: _____

Awakened Time: _____

Sleep Duration: _____

Toss & Turned: ☐ yes ☐ no

Cold: ☐ yes ☐ no

Hot: ☐ yes ☐ no

CATEGORY

☐ Premonition ☐ Ancestral ☐ Subconscious ☐ Employment
☐ Current/Past Event ☐ Abuse ☐ Trauma ☐ Nudity
☐ Sexual ☐ Family ☐ Not Sure

Something Else: _____

ATTRIBUTES

☐ Colorful ☐ Black & White ☐ Loud/Noisy ☐ Quiet ☐ Sunny
☐ Dark ☐ Water ☐ Earth/Dirt ☐ Fire ☐ Sky
☐ Wind/Tornado ☐ Cold ☐ Hot ☐ Wet ☐ Not Sure

Something Else: _____

CHARACTERS

☐ People ☐ Animals ☐ Spirits
☐ Angels ☐ Demons ☐ Gods
☐ Not Sure ☐ None

Something Else: _____

EMOTIONS

☐ Anger ☐ Love ☐ Guilt ☐ Sadness
☐ Jealousy ☐ Confusion ☐ Grief ☐ Happiness
☐ Fear ☐ Shock ☐ Courage ☐ Not Sure

Something Else: _____

JOURNAL

_____
_____
_____
_____
_____
_____
_____
_____
_____
_____
_____
_____
_____
_____
_____
_____
_____
_____
_____
_____
_____
_____
_____
_____

SPECIAL NOTES

_____
_____
_____
_____

Date: _____

Bed Time: _____
Awakened Time: _____
Sleep Duration: _____

Toss & Turned: ☐ yes ☐ no
Cold: ☐ yes ☐ no
Hot: ☐ yes ☐ no

CATEGORY

☐ Premonition ☐ Ancestral ☐ Subconscious ☐ Employment
☐ Current/Past Event ☐ Abuse ☐ Trauma ☐ Nudity
☐ Sexual ☐ Family ☐ Not Sure

Something Else: _____

ATTRIBUTES

☐ Colorful ☐ Black & White ☐ Loud/Noisy ☐ Quiet ☐ Sunny
☐ Dark ☐ Water ☐ Earth/Dirt ☐ Fire ☐ Sky
☐ Wind/Tornado ☐ Cold ☐ Hot ☐ Wet ☐ Not Sure

Something Else: _____

CHARACTERS

☐ People ☐ Animals ☐ Spirits
☐ Angels ☐ Demons ☐ Gods
☐ Not Sure ☐ None Something Else: _____

EMOTIONS

☐ Anger ☐ Love ☐ Guilt ☐ Sadness
☐ Jealousy ☐ Confusion ☐ Grief ☐ Happiness
☐ Fear ☐ Shock ☐ Courage ☐ Not Sure

Something Else: _____

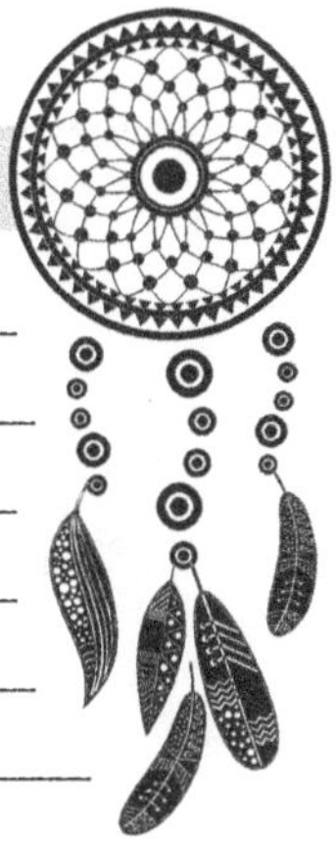

JOURNAL

_____

_____

_____

_____

_____

_____

_____

_____

_____

_____

_____

_____

_____

_____

_____

_____

_____

_____

_____

_____

_____

_____

_____

SPECIAL NOTES

_____

_____

_____

_____

Date: _____

Bed Time: _____

Awakened Time: _____

Sleep Duration: _____

Toss & Turned: ☐ yes ☐ no

Cold: ☐ yes ☐ no

Hot: ☐ yes ☐ no

CATEGORY

☐ Premonition
☐ Current/Past Event
☐ Sexual

☐ Ancestral
☐ Abuse
☐ Family

☐ Subconscious
☐ Trauma
☐ Not Sure

☐ Employment
☐ Nudity

Something Else: _____

ATTRIBUTES

☐ Colorful
☐ Dark
☐ Wind/Tornado

☐ Black & White
☐ Water
☐ Cold

☐ Loud/Noisy
☐ Earth/Dirt
☐ Hot

☐ Quiet
☐ Fire
☐ Wet

☐ Sunny
☐ Sky
☐ Not Sure

Something Else: _____

CHARACTERS

☐ People
☐ Angels
☐ Not Sure

☐ Animals
☐ Demons
☐ None

☐ Spirits
☐ Gods

Something Else: _____

EMOTIONS

☐ Anger
☐ Jealousy
☐ Fear

☐ Love
☐ Confusion
☐ Shock

☐ Guilt
☐ Grief
☐ Courage

☐ Sadness
☐ Happiness
☐ Not Sure

Something Else: _____

JOURNAL

_____
_____
_____
_____
_____
_____
_____
_____
_____
_____
_____
_____
_____
_____
_____
_____
_____
_____
_____
_____
_____
_____
_____
_____

SPECIAL NOTES

_____
_____
_____
_____

Bed Time: _____

Awakened Time: _____

Sleep Duration: _____

Toss & Turned: ☐ yes ☐ no

Cold: ☐ yes ☐ no

Hot: ☐ yes ☐ no

CATEGORY

☐ Premonition ☐ Ancestral ☐ Subconscious ☐ Employment
☐ Current/Past Event ☐ Abuse ☐ Trauma ☐ Nudity
☐ Sexual ☐ Family ☐ Not Sure

Something Else: _____

ATTRIBUTES

☐ Colorful ☐ Black & White ☐ Loud/Noisy ☐ Quiet ☐ Sunny
☐ Dark ☐ Water ☐ Earth/Dirt ☐ Fire ☐ Sky
☐ Wind/Tornado ☐ Cold ☐ Hot ☐ Wet ☐ Not Sure

Something Else: _____

CHARACTERS

☐ People ☐ Animals ☐ Spirits
☐ Angels ☐ Demons ☐ Gods
☐ Not Sure ☐ None Something Else: _____

EMOTIONS

☐ Anger ☐ Love ☐ Guilt ☐ Sadness
☐ Jealousy ☐ Confusion ☐ Grief ☐ Happiness
☐ Fear ☐ Shock ☐ Courage ☐ Not Sure

Something Else: _____

JOURNAL

_____
_____
_____
_____
_____
_____
_____
_____
_____
_____
_____
_____
_____
_____
_____
_____
_____
_____
_____
_____
_____
_____
_____
_____
_____

SPECIAL NOTES

_____
_____
_____
_____

Date: _____

Bed Time: _____
Awakened Time: _____
Sleep Duration: _____

Toss & Turned: ☐ yes ☐ no
Cold: ☐ yes ☐ no
Hot: ☐ yes ☐ no

CATEGORY

☐ Premonition   ☐ Ancestral   ☐ Subconscious   ☐ Employment
☐ Current/Past Event ☐ Abuse   ☐ Trauma   ☐ Nudity
☐ Sexual   ☐ Family   ☐ Not Sure

Something Else: _____

ATTRIBUTES

☐ Colorful   ☐ Black & White   ☐ Loud/Noisy   ☐ Quiet   ☐ Sunny
☐ Dark   ☐ Water   ☐ Earth/Dirt   ☐ Fire   ☐ Sky
☐ Wind/Tornado   ☐ Cold   ☐ Hot   ☐ Wet   ☐ Not Sure

Something Else: _____

CHARACTERS

☐ People   ☐ Animals   ☐ Spirits
☐ Angels   ☐ Demons   ☐ Gods
☐ Not Sure   ☐ None   Something Else: _____

EMOTIONS

☐ Anger   ☐ Love   ☐ Guilt   ☐ Sadness
☐ Jealousy   ☐ Confusion   ☐ Grief   ☐ Happiness
☐ Fear   ☐ Shock   ☐ Courage   ☐ Not Sure

Something Else: _____

JOURNAL

_____
_____
_____
_____
_____
_____
_____
_____
_____
_____
_____
_____
_____
_____
_____
_____
_____
_____
_____
_____
_____
_____

SPECIAL NOTES

_____
_____
_____
_____

Date: _____

Bed Time: _____   Toss & Turned: ☐ yes ☐ no
Awakened Time: _____   Cold: ☐ yes ☐ no
Sleep Duration: _____   Hot: ☐ yes ☐ no

CATEGORY

☐ Premonition   ☐ Ancestral   ☐ Subconscious   ☐ Employment
☐ Current/Past Event   ☐ Abuse   ☐ Trauma   ☐ Nudity
☐ Sexual   ☐ Family   ☐ Not Sure

Something Else: _____

ATTRIBUTES

☐ Colorful   ☐ Black & White   ☐ Loud/Noisy   ☐ Quiet   ☐ Sunny
☐ Dark   ☐ Water   ☐ Earth/Dirt   ☐ Fire   ☐ Sky
☐ Wind/Tornado   ☐ Cold   ☐ Hot   ☐ Wet   ☐ Not Sure

Something Else: _____

CHARACTERS

☐ People   ☐ Animals   ☐ Spirits
☐ Angels   ☐ Demons   ☐ Gods
☐ Not Sure   ☐ None   Something Else: _____

EMOTIONS

☐ Anger   ☐ Love   ☐ Guilt   ☐ Sadness
☐ Jealousy   ☐ Confusion   ☐ Grief   ☐ Happiness
☐ Fear   ☐ Shock   ☐ Courage   ☐ Not Sure

Something Else: _____

JOURNAL

SPECIAL NOTES

Date: _____

Bed Time: _____

Awakened Time: _____

Sleep Duration: _____

Toss & Turned: ☐ yes ☐ no

Cold: ☐ yes ☐ no

Hot: ☐ yes ☐ no

CATEGORY

☐ Premonition   ☐ Ancestral   ☐ Subconscious   ☐ Employment

☐ Current/Past Event ☐ Abuse   ☐ Trauma   ☐ Nudity

☐ Sexual   ☐ Family   ☐ Not Sure

Something Else: _____

ATTRIBUTES

☐ Colorful   ☐ Black & White   ☐ Loud/Noisy   ☐ Quiet   ☐ Sunny

☐ Dark   ☐ Water   ☐ Earth/Dirt   ☐ Fire   ☐ Sky

☐ Wind/Tornado   ☐ Cold   ☐ Hot   ☐ Wet   ☐ Not Sure

Something Else: _____

CHARACTERS

☐ People   ☐ Animals   ☐ Spirits

☐ Angels   ☐ Demons   ☐ Gods

☐ Not Sure   ☐ None   Something Else: _____

EMOTIONS

☐ Anger   ☐ Love   ☐ Guilt   ☐ Sadness

☐ Jealousy   ☐ Confusion   ☐ Grief   ☐ Happiness

☐ Fear   ☐ Shock   ☐ Courage   ☐ Not Sure

Something Else: _____

_____
_____
_____
_____
_____
_____
_____
_____
_____
_____
_____
_____
_____
_____
_____
_____
_____
_____
_____
_____
_____
_____
_____
_____

SPECIAL NOTES

_____
_____
_____
_____

Date: _____

Bed Time: _____ Toss & Turned: ☐ yes ☐ no

Awakened Time: _____ Cold: ☐ yes ☐ no

Sleep Duration: _____ Hot: ☐ yes ☐ no

CATEGORY

☐ Premonition ☐ Ancestral ☐ Subconscious ☐ Employment

☐ Current/Past Event ☐ Abuse ☐ Trauma ☐ Nudity

☐ Sexual ☐ Family ☐ Not Sure

Something Else: _____

ATTRIBUTES

☐ Colorful ☐ Black & White ☐ Loud/Noisy ☐ Quiet ☐ Sunny

☐ Dark ☐ Water ☐ Earth/Dirt ☐ Fire ☐ Sky

☐ Wind/Tornado ☐ Cold ☐ Hot ☐ Wet ☐ Not Sure

Something Else: _____

CHARACTERS

☐ People ☐ Animals ☐ Spirits

☐ Angels ☐ Demons ☐ Gods

☐ Not Sure ☐ None Something Else: _____

EMOTIONS

☐ Anger ☐ Love ☐ Guilt ☐ Sadness

☐ Jealousy ☐ Confusion ☐ Grief ☐ Happiness

☐ Fear ☐ Shock ☐ Courage ☐ Not Sure

Something Else: _____

JOURNAL

_____
_____
_____
_____
_____
_____
_____
_____
_____
_____
_____
_____
_____
_____
_____
_____
_____
_____
_____
_____
_____
_____
_____

SPECIAL NOTES

_____
_____
_____
_____

Date: _____

Bed Time: _____   Toss & Turned: ☐ yes ☐ no

Awakened Time: _____   Cold: ☐ yes ☐ no

Sleep Duration: _____   Hot: ☐ yes ☐ no

CATEGORY

☐ Premonition   ☐ Ancestral   ☐ Subconscious   ☐ Employment

☐ Current/Past Event   ☐ Abuse   ☐ Trauma   ☐ Nudity

☐ Sexual   ☐ Family   ☐ Not Sure

Something Else: _____

ATTRIBUTES

☐ Colorful   ☐ Black & White   ☐ Loud/Noisy   ☐ Quiet   ☐ Sunny

☐ Dark   ☐ Water   ☐ Earth/Dirt   ☐ Fire   ☐ Sky

☐ Wind/Tornado   ☐ Cold   ☐ Hot   ☐ Wet   ☐ Not Sure

Something Else: _____

CHARACTERS

☐ People   ☐ Animals   ☐ Spirits

☐ Angels   ☐ Demons   ☐ Gods

☐ Not Sure   ☐ None   Something Else: _____

EMOTIONS

☐ Anger   ☐ Love   ☐ Guilt   ☐ Sadness

☐ Jealousy   ☐ Confusion   ☐ Grief   ☐ Happiness

☐ Fear   ☐ Shock   ☐ Courage   ☐ Not Sure

Something Else: _____

_____
_____
_____
_____
_____
_____
_____
_____
_____
_____
_____
_____
_____
_____
_____
_____
_____
_____
_____
_____
_____
_____
_____
_____

SPECIAL NOTES

_____
_____
_____
_____

_____ _____

Date: _____

Bed Time: _____   Toss & Turned: ☐ yes ☐ no

Awakened Time: _____   Cold: ☐ yes ☐ no

Sleep Duration: _____   Hot: ☐ yes ☐ no

CATEGORY

☐ Premonition   ☐ Ancestral   ☐ Subconscious   ☐ Employment

☐ Current/Past Event   ☐ Abuse   ☐ Trauma   ☐ Nudity

☐ Sexual   ☐ Family   ☐ Not Sure

Something Else: _____

ATTRIBUTES

☐ Colorful   ☐ Black & White   ☐ Loud/Noisy   ☐ Quiet   ☐ Sunny

☐ Dark   ☐ Water   ☐ Earth/Dirt   ☐ Fire   ☐ Sky

☐ Wind/Tornado   ☐ Cold   ☐ Hot   ☐ Wet   ☐ Not Sure

Something Else: _____

CHARACTERS

☐ People   ☐ Animals   ☐ Spirits

☐ Angels   ☐ Demons   ☐ Gods

☐ Not Sure   ☐ None   Something Else: _____

EMOTIONS

☐ Anger   ☐ Love   ☐ Guilt   ☐ Sadness

☐ Jealousy   ☐ Confusion   ☐ Grief   ☐ Happiness

☐ Fear   ☐ Shock   ☐ Courage   ☐ Not Sure

Something Else: _____

JOURNAL

_____
_____
_____
_____
_____
_____
_____
_____
_____
_____
_____
_____
_____
_____
_____
_____
_____
_____
_____
_____
_____
_____
_____
_____

SPECIAL NOTES

_____
_____
_____
_____

Date: _____

Bed Time: _____
Awakened Time: _____
Sleep Duration: _____

Toss & Turned: ☐ yes ☐ no
Cold: ☐ yes ☐ no
Hot: ☐ yes ☐ no

CATEGORY

☐ Premonition
☐ Current/Past Event
☐ Sexual

☐ Ancestral
☐ Abuse
☐ Family

☐ Subconscious
☐ Trauma
☐ Not Sure

☐ Employment
☐ Nudity

Something Else: _____

ATTRIBUTES

☐ Colorful
☐ Dark
☐ Wind/Tornado

☐ Black & White
☐ Water
☐ Cold

☐ Loud/Noisy
☐ Earth/Dirt
☐ Hot

☐ Quiet
☐ Fire
☐ Wet

☐ Sunny
☐ Sky
☐ Not Sure

Something Else: _____

CHARACTERS

☐ People
☐ Angels
☐ Not Sure

☐ Animals
☐ Demons
☐ None

☐ Spirits
☐ Gods

Something Else: _____

EMOTIONS

☐ Anger
☐ Jealousy
☐ Fear

☐ Love
☐ Confusion
☐ Shock

☐ Guilt
☐ Grief
☐ Courage

☐ Sadness
☐ Happiness
☐ Not Sure

Something Else: _____

JOURNAL

_____
_____
_____
_____
_____
_____
_____
_____
_____
_____
_____
_____
_____
_____
_____
_____
_____
_____
_____
_____
_____
_____
_____

SPECIAL NOTES

_____
_____
_____
_____

_____   _____

Date: _____

Bed Time: _____   Toss & Turned: ☐ yes ☐ no

Awakened Time: _____   Cold: ☐ yes ☐ no

Sleep Duration: _____   Hot: ☐ yes ☐ no

CATEGORY

☐ Premonition   ☐ Ancestral   ☐ Subconscious   ☐ Employment

☐ Current/Past Event ☐ Abuse   ☐ Trauma   ☐ Nudity

☐ Sexual   ☐ Family   ☐ Not Sure

Something Else: _____

ATTRIBUTES

☐ Colorful   ☐ Black & White   ☐ Loud/Noisy   ☐ Quiet   ☐ Sunny

☐ Dark   ☐ Water   ☐ Earth/Dirt   ☐ Fire   ☐ Sky

☐ Wind/Tornado   ☐ Cold   ☐ Hot   ☐ Wet   ☐ Not Sure

Something Else: _____

CHARACTERS

☐ People   ☐ Animals   ☐ Spirits

☐ Angels   ☐ Demons   ☐ Gods

☐ Not Sure   ☐ None   Something Else: _____

EMOTIONS

☐ Anger   ☐ Love   ☐ Guilt   ☐ Sadness

☐ Jealousy   ☐ Confusion   ☐ Grief   ☐ Happiness

☐ Fear   ☐ Shock   ☐ Courage   ☐ Not Sure

Something Else: _____

JOURNAL

SPECIAL NOTES

Date: _____

Bed Time: _____

Awakened Time: _____

Sleep Duration: _____

Toss & Turned: ☐ yes ☐ no

Cold: ☐ yes ☐ no

Hot: ☐ yes ☐ no

CATEGORY

☐ Premonition ☐ Ancestral ☐ Subconscious ☐ Employment
☐ Current/Past Event ☐ Abuse ☐ Trauma ☐ Nudity
☐ Sexual ☐ Family ☐ Not Sure

Something Else: _____

ATTRIBUTES

☐ Colorful ☐ Black & White ☐ Loud/Noisy ☐ Quiet ☐ Sunny
☐ Dark ☐ Water ☐ Earth/Dirt ☐ Fire ☐ Sky
☐ Wind/Tornado ☐ Cold ☐ Hot ☐ Wet ☐ Not Sure

Something Else: _____

CHARACTERS

☐ People ☐ Animals ☐ Spirits
☐ Angels ☐ Demons ☐ Gods
☐ Not Sure ☐ None Something Else: _____

EMOTIONS

☐ Anger ☐ Love ☐ Guilt ☐ Sadness
☐ Jealousy ☐ Confusion ☐ Grief ☐ Happiness
☐ Fear ☐ Shock ☐ Courage ☐ Not Sure

Something Else: _____

JOURNAL

_____
_____
_____
_____
_____
_____
_____
_____
_____
_____
_____
_____
_____
_____
_____
_____
_____
_____
_____
_____
_____
_____
_____
_____

SPECIAL NOTES

_____
_____
_____
_____

Date: _____

Bed Time: _____

Awakened Time: _____

Sleep Duration: _____

Toss & Turned: ☐ yes ☐ no

Cold: ☐ yes ☐ no

Hot: ☐ yes ☐ no

CATEGORY

☐ Premonition
☐ Current/Past Event
☐ Sexual

☐ Ancestral
☐ Abuse
☐ Family

☐ Subconscious
☐ Trauma
☐ Not Sure

☐ Employment
☐ Nudity

Something Else: _____

ATTRIBUTES

☐ Colorful
☐ Dark
☐ Wind/Tornado

☐ Black & White
☐ Water
☐ Cold

☐ Loud/Noisy
☐ Earth/Dirt
☐ Hot

☐ Quiet
☐ Fire
☐ Wet

☐ Sunny
☐ Sky
☐ Not Sure

Something Else: _____

CHARACTERS

☐ People
☐ Angels
☐ Not Sure

☐ Animals
☐ Demons
☐ None

☐ Spirits
☐ Gods

Something Else: _____

EMOTIONS

☐ Anger
☐ Jealousy
☐ Fear

☐ Love
☐ Confusion
☐ Shock

☐ Guilt
☐ Grief
☐ Courage

☐ Sadness
☐ Happiness
☐ Not Sure

Something Else: _____

JOURNAL

_____
_____
_____
_____
_____
_____
_____
_____
_____
_____
_____
_____
_____
_____
_____
_____
_____
_____
_____
_____
_____
_____
_____
_____
_____

SPECIAL NOTES

_____
_____
_____
_____

Date: _____

Bed Time: _____

Awakened Time: _____

Sleep Duration: _____

Toss & Turned: ☐ yes ☐ no

Cold: ☐ yes ☐ no

Hot: ☐ yes ☐ no

CATEGORY

☐ Premonition ☐ Ancestral ☐ Subconscious ☐ Employment

☐ Current/Past Event ☐ Abuse ☐ Trauma ☐ Nudity

☐ Sexual ☐ Family ☐ Not Sure

Something Else: _____

ATTRIBUTES

☐ Colorful ☐ Black & White ☐ Loud/Noisy ☐ Quiet ☐ Sunny

☐ Dark ☐ Water ☐ Earth/Dirt ☐ Fire ☐ Sky

☐ Wind/Tornado ☐ Cold ☐ Hot ☐ Wet ☐ Not Sure

Something Else: _____

CHARACTERS

☐ People ☐ Animals ☐ Spirits

☐ Angels ☐ Demons ☐ Gods

☐ Not Sure ☐ None Something Else: _____

EMOTIONS

☐ Anger ☐ Love ☐ Guilt ☐ Sadness

☐ Jealousy ☐ Confusion ☐ Grief ☐ Happiness

☐ Fear ☐ Shock ☐ Courage ☐ Not Sure

Something Else: _____

JOURNAL

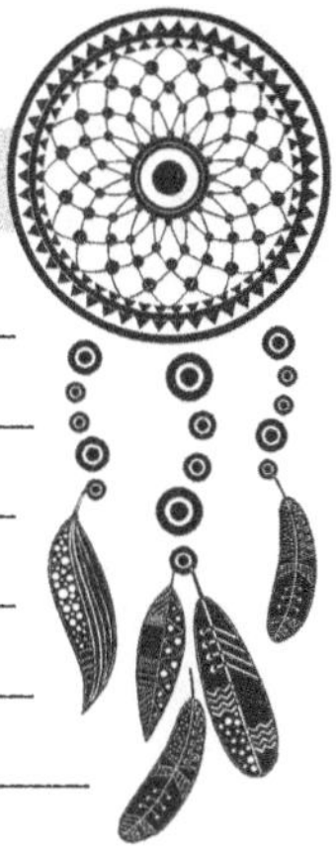

_____
_____
_____
_____
_____
_____
_____
_____
_____
_____
_____
_____
_____
_____
_____
_____
_____
_____
_____
_____
_____
_____
_____
_____

SPECIAL NOTES

_____
_____
_____
_____

Date: _____

Bed Time: _____   Toss & Turned: ☐ yes ☐ no

Awakened Time: _____   Cold: ☐ yes ☐ no

Sleep Duration: _____   Hot: ☐ yes ☐ no

CATEGORY

☐ Premonition   ☐ Ancestral   ☐ Subconscious   ☐ Employment

☐ Current/Past Event   ☐ Abuse   ☐ Trauma   ☐ Nudity

☐ Sexual   ☐ Family   ☐ Not Sure

Something Else: _____

ATTRIBUTES

☐ Colorful   ☐ Black & White   ☐ Loud/Noisy   ☐ Quiet   ☐ Sunny

☐ Dark   ☐ Water   ☐ Earth/Dirt   ☐ Fire   ☐ Sky

☐ Wind/Tornado   ☐ Cold   ☐ Hot   ☐ Wet   ☐ Not Sure

Something Else: _____

CHARACTERS

☐ People   ☐ Animals   ☐ Spirits

☐ Angels   ☐ Demons   ☐ Gods

☐ Not Sure   ☐ None   Something Else: _____

EMOTIONS

☐ Anger   ☐ Love   ☐ Guilt   ☐ Sadness

☐ Jealousy   ☐ Confusion   ☐ Grief   ☐ Happiness

☐ Fear   ☐ Shock   ☐ Courage   ☐ Not Sure

Something Else: _____

JOURNAL

SPECIAL NOTES

Date: _____

Bed Time: _____   Toss & Turned: ☐ yes ☐ no

Awakened Time: _____   Cold: ☐ yes ☐ no

Sleep Duration: _____   Hot: ☐ yes ☐ no

CATEGORY

☐ Premonition   ☐ Ancestral   ☐ Subconscious   ☐ Employment

☐ Current/Past Event   ☐ Abuse   ☐ Trauma   ☐ Nudity

☐ Sexual   ☐ Family   ☐ Not Sure

Something Else: _____

ATTRIBUTES

☐ Colorful   ☐ Black & White   ☐ Loud/Noisy   ☐ Quiet   ☐ Sunny

☐ Dark   ☐ Water   ☐ Earth/Dirt   ☐ Fire   ☐ Sky

☐ Wind/Tornado   ☐ Cold   ☐ Hot   ☐ Wet   ☐ Not Sure

Something Else: _____

CHARACTERS

☐ People   ☐ Animals   ☐ Spirits

☐ Angels   ☐ Demons   ☐ Gods

☐ Not Sure   ☐ None   Something Else: _____

EMOTIONS

☐ Anger   ☐ Love   ☐ Guilt   ☐ Sadness

☐ Jealousy   ☐ Confusion   ☐ Grief   ☐ Happiness

☐ Fear   ☐ Shock   ☐ Courage   ☐ Not Sure

Something Else: _____

JOURNAL

_____
_____
_____
_____
_____
_____
_____
_____
_____
_____
_____
_____
_____
_____
_____
_____
_____
_____
_____
_____
_____
_____
_____
_____

SPECIAL NOTES

_____
_____
_____
_____
_____

Date: _____

Bed Time: _____   Toss & Turned: ☐ yes ☐ no

Awakened Time: _____   Cold: ☐ yes ☐ no

Sleep Duration: _____   Hot: ☐ yes ☐ no

CATEGORY

☐ Premonition   ☐ Ancestral   ☐ Subconscious   ☐ Employment

☐ Current/Past Event   ☐ Abuse   ☐ Trauma   ☐ Nudity

☐ Sexual   ☐ Family   ☐ Not Sure

Something Else: _____

ATTRIBUTES

☐ Colorful   ☐ Black & White   ☐ Loud/Noisy   ☐ Quiet   ☐ Sunny

☐ Dark   ☐ Water   ☐ Earth/Dirt   ☐ Fire   ☐ Sky

☐ Wind/Tornado   ☐ Cold   ☐ Hot   ☐ Wet   ☐ Not Sure

Something Else: _____

CHARACTERS

☐ People   ☐ Animals   ☐ Spirits

☐ Angels   ☐ Demons   ☐ Gods

☐ Not Sure   ☐ None   Something Else: _____

EMOTIONS

☐ Anger   ☐ Love   ☐ Guilt   ☐ Sadness

☐ Jealousy   ☐ Confusion   ☐ Grief   ☐ Happiness

☐ Fear   ☐ Shock   ☐ Courage   ☐ Not Sure

Something Else: _____

JOURNAL

_____
_____
_____
_____
_____
_____
_____
_____
_____
_____
_____
_____
_____
_____
_____
_____
_____
_____
_____
_____
_____
_____
_____

SPECIAL NOTES

_____
_____
_____
_____

Date: _____

Bed Time: _____

Awakened Time: _____

Sleep Duration: _____

Toss & Turned: ☐ yes ☐ no

Cold: ☐ yes ☐ no

Hot: ☐ yes ☐ no

CATEGORY

☐ Premonition
☐ Current/Past Event
☐ Sexual

☐ Ancestral
☐ Abuse
☐ Family

☐ Subconscious
☐ Trauma
☐ Not Sure

☐ Employment
☐ Nudity

Something Else: _____

ATTRIBUTES

☐ Colorful
☐ Dark
☐ Wind/Tornado

☐ Black & White
☐ Water
☐ Cold

☐ Loud/Noisy
☐ Earth/Dirt
☐ Hot

☐ Quiet
☐ Fire
☐ Wet

☐ Sunny
☐ Sky
☐ Not Sure

Something Else: _____

CHARACTERS

☐ People
☐ Angels
☐ Not Sure

☐ Animals
☐ Demons
☐ None

☐ Spirits
☐ Gods

Something Else: _____

EMOTIONS

☐ Anger
☐ Jealousy
☐ Fear

☐ Love
☐ Confusion
☐ Shock

☐ Guilt
☐ Grief
☐ Courage

☐ Sadness
☐ Happiness
☐ Not Sure

Something Else: _____

_____
_____
_____
_____
_____
_____
_____
_____
_____
_____
_____
_____
_____
_____
_____
_____
_____
_____
_____
_____
_____
_____

SPECIAL NOTES

_____
_____
_____
_____

Date: _____

Bed Time: _____   Toss & Turned: ☐ yes ☐ no
Awakened Time: _____   Cold: ☐ yes ☐ no
Sleep Duration: _____   Hot: ☐ yes ☐ no

CATEGORY

☐ Premonition   ☐ Ancestral   ☐ Subconscious   ☐ Employment
☐ Current/Past Event   ☐ Abuse   ☐ Trauma   ☐ Nudity
☐ Sexual   ☐ Family   ☐ Not Sure

Something Else: _____

ATTRIBUTES

☐ Colorful   ☐ Black & White   ☐ Loud/Noisy   ☐ Quiet   ☐ Sunny
☐ Dark   ☐ Water   ☐ Earth/Dirt   ☐ Fire   ☐ Sky
☐ Wind/Tornado   ☐ Cold   ☐ Hot   ☐ Wet   ☐ Not Sure

Something Else: _____

CHARACTERS

☐ People   ☐ Animals   ☐ Spirits
☐ Angels   ☐ Demons   ☐ Gods
☐ Not Sure   ☐ None   Something Else: _____

EMOTIONS

☐ Anger   ☐ Love   ☐ Guilt   ☐ Sadness
☐ Jealousy   ☐ Confusion   ☐ Grief   ☐ Happiness
☐ Fear   ☐ Shock   ☐ Courage   ☐ Not Sure

Something Else: _____

JOURNAL

SPECIAL NOTES

Date: _____

Bed Time: _____   Toss & Turned: ☐ yes ☐ no

Awakened Time: _____   Cold: ☐ yes ☐ no

Sleep Duration: _____   Hot: ☐ yes ☐ no

CATEGORY

☐ Premonition   ☐ Ancestral   ☐ Subconscious   ☐ Employment

☐ Current/Past Event   ☐ Abuse   ☐ Trauma   ☐ Nudity

☐ Sexual   ☐ Family   ☐ Not Sure

Something Else: _____

ATTRIBUTES

☐ Colorful   ☐ Black & White   ☐ Loud/Noisy   ☐ Quiet   ☐ Sunny

☐ Dark   ☐ Water   ☐ Earth/Dirt   ☐ Fire   ☐ Sky

☐ Wind/Tornado   ☐ Cold   ☐ Hot   ☐ Wet   ☐ Not Sure

Something Else: _____

CHARACTERS

☐ People   ☐ Animals   ☐ Spirits

☐ Angels   ☐ Demons   ☐ Gods

☐ Not Sure   ☐ None   Something Else: _____

EMOTIONS

☐ Anger   ☐ Love   ☐ Guilt   ☐ Sadness

☐ Jealousy   ☐ Confusion   ☐ Grief   ☐ Happiness

☐ Fear   ☐ Shock   ☐ Courage   ☐ Not Sure

Something Else: _____

_____
_____
_____
_____
_____
_____
_____
_____
_____
_____
_____
_____
_____
_____
_____
_____
_____
_____
_____
_____
_____
_____
_____
_____

SPECIAL NOTES

_____
_____
_____
_____
_____

Date: _____

Bed Time: _____
Awakened Time: _____
Sleep Duration: _____

Toss & Turned: ☐ yes ☐ no
Cold: ☐ yes ☐ no
Hot: ☐ yes ☐ no

CATEGORY

☐ Premonition ☐ Ancestral ☐ Subconscious ☐ Employment
☐ Current/Past Event ☐ Abuse ☐ Trauma ☐ Nudity
☐ Sexual ☐ Family ☐ Not Sure

Something Else: _____

ATTRIBUTES

☐ Colorful ☐ Black & White ☐ Loud/Noisy ☐ Quiet ☐ Sunny
☐ Dark ☐ Water ☐ Earth/Dirt ☐ Fire ☐ Sky
☐ Wind/Tornado ☐ Cold ☐ Hot ☐ Wet ☐ Not Sure

Something Else: _____

CHARACTERS

☐ People ☐ Animals ☐ Spirits
☐ Angels ☐ Demons ☐ Gods
☐ Not Sure ☐ None

Something Else: _____

EMOTIONS

☐ Anger ☐ Love ☐ Guilt ☐ Sadness
☐ Jealousy ☐ Confusion ☐ Grief ☐ Happiness
☐ Fear ☐ Shock ☐ Courage ☐ Not Sure

Something Else: _____

JOURNAL

_____
_____
_____
_____
_____
_____
_____
_____
_____
_____
_____
_____
_____
_____
_____
_____
_____
_____
_____
_____
_____
_____
_____
_____
_____
_____

SPECIAL NOTES

_____
_____
_____
_____

Date: _____

Bed Time: _____

Awakened Time: _____

Sleep Duration: _____

Toss & Turned: ☐ yes ☐ no

Cold: ☐ yes ☐ no

Hot: ☐ yes ☐ no

CATEGORY

☐ Premonition
☐ Current/Past Event
☐ Sexual

☐ Ancestral
☐ Abuse
☐ Family

☐ Subconscious
☐ Trauma
☐ Not Sure

☐ Employment
☐ Nudity

Something Else: _____

ATTRIBUTES

☐ Colorful
☐ Dark
☐ Wind/Tornado

☐ Black & White
☐ Water
☐ Cold

☐ Loud/Noisy
☐ Earth/Dirt
☐ Hot

☐ Quiet
☐ Fire
☐ Wet

☐ Sunny
☐ Sky
☐ Not Sure

Something Else: _____

CHARACTERS

☐ People
☐ Angels
☐ Not Sure

☐ Animals
☐ Demons
☐ None

☐ Spirits
☐ Gods

Something Else: _____

EMOTIONS

☐ Anger
☐ Jealousy
☐ Fear

☐ Love
☐ Confusion
☐ Shock

☐ Guilt
☐ Grief
☐ Courage

☐ Sadness
☐ Happiness
☐ Not Sure

Something Else: _____

JOURNAL

_____
_____
_____
_____
_____
_____
_____
_____
_____
_____
_____
_____
_____
_____
_____
_____
_____
_____
_____
_____
_____
_____

SPECIAL NOTES

_____
_____
_____
_____

ADDITIONAL NOTES

ADDITIONAL NOTES

ADDITIONAL NOTES

ADDITIONAL NOTES

ADDITIONAL NOTES

ADDITIONAL NOTES

ADDITIONAL NOTES

ADDITIONAL NOTES

ADDITIONAL NOTES

ADDITIONAL NOTES

ADDITIONAL WORKS
BY AUTHOR

An Alchemist
Journey in Scent

Totukani Amen II

An Alchemist Journey in Scent
Author's Life Story

ADDITIONAL WORKS
BY AUTHOR

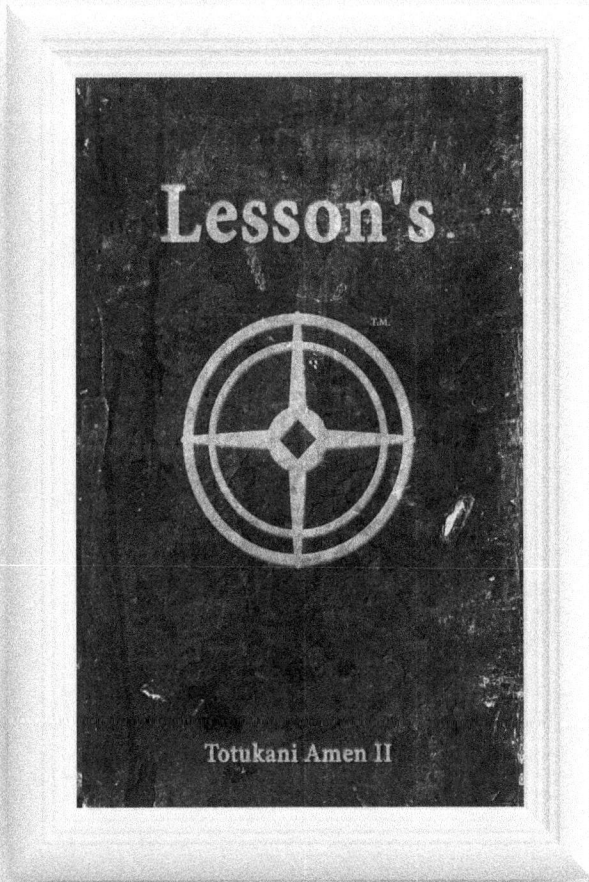

Book I–Lessons
Karma Release and Internal Power Generation

ADDITIONAL WORKS
BY AUTHOR

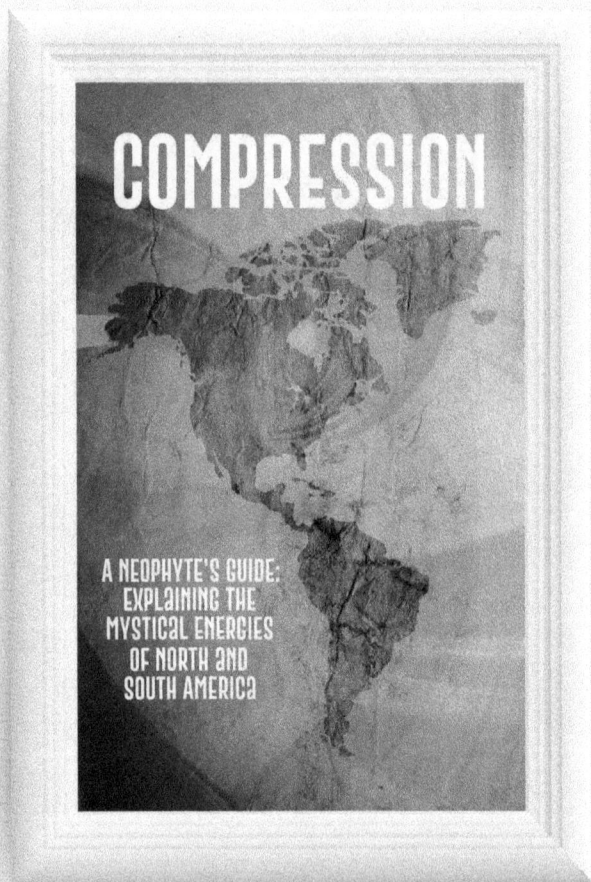

Compression
A Neophytes Guide to the
Mystical Energies of North and South America

ADDITIONAL WORKS
BY AUTHOR

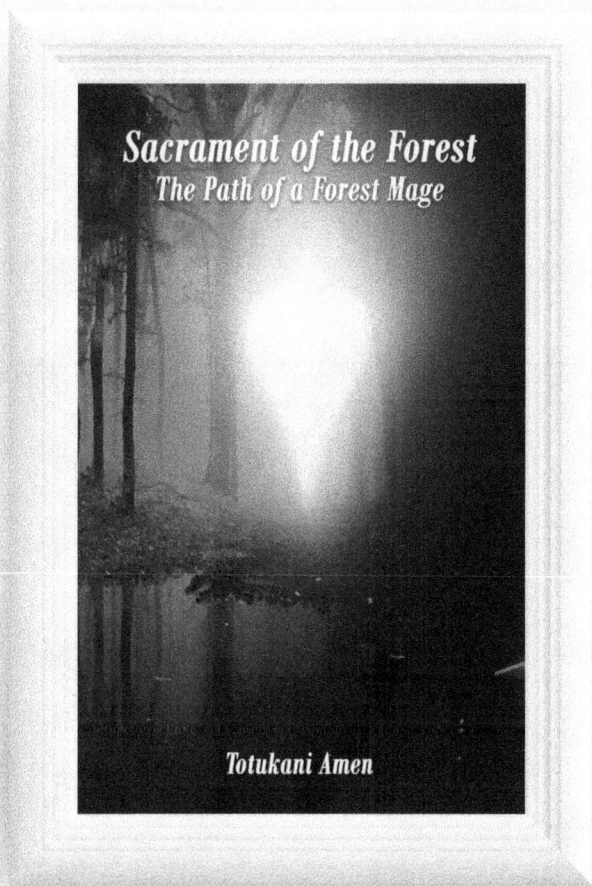

Sacrament of the Forest
How to become a Guardian of the Forest

ADDITIONAL WORKS
BY AUTHOR

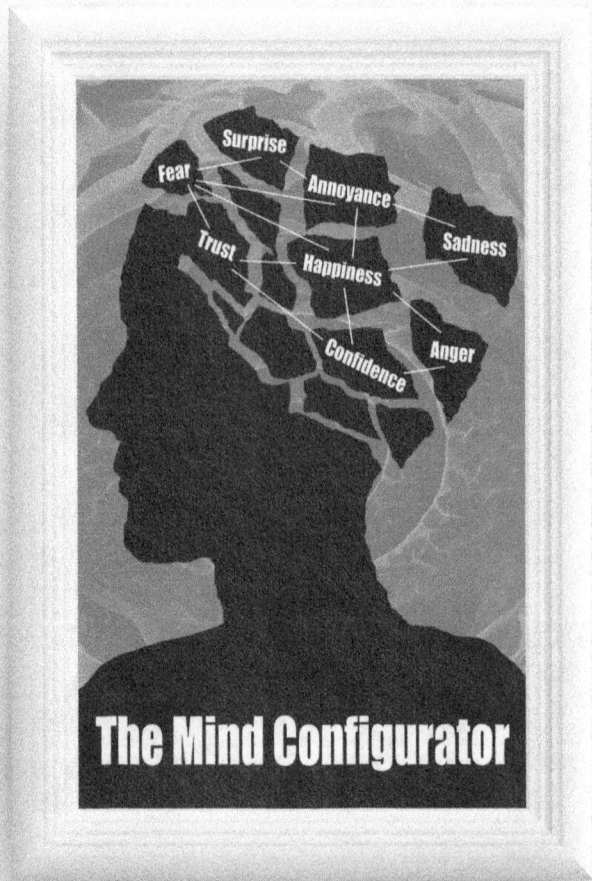

The Mind Configurator
Advanced Technique to access the Subconscious Mind

ADDITIONAL WORKS
BY AUTHOR

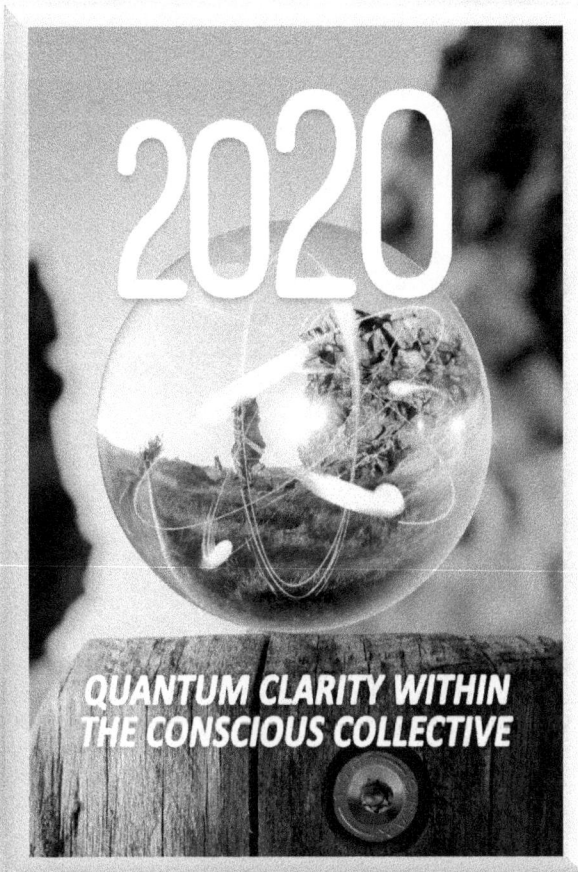

2020
Quantum Clarity within the Conscious Collective

ADDITIONAL WORKS
BY AUTHOR

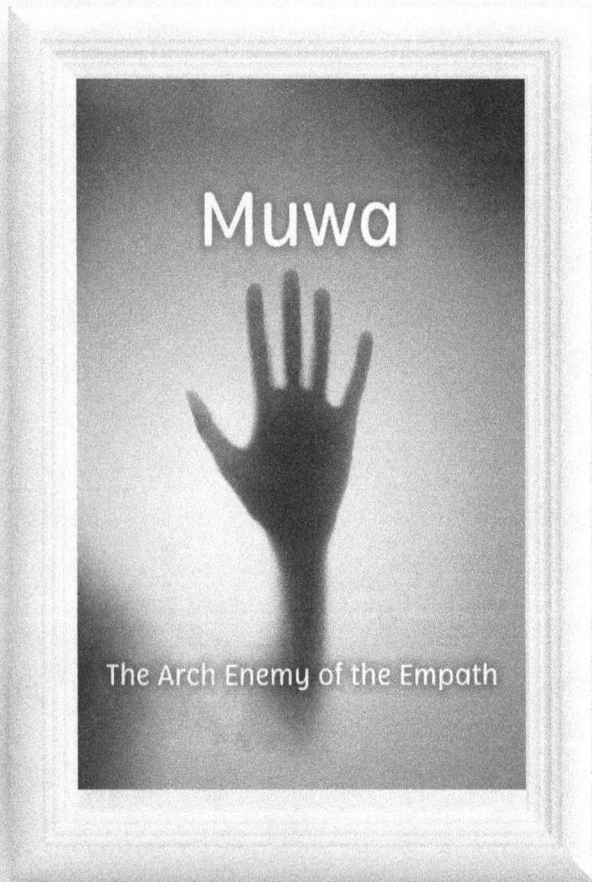

Muwa
The Arch Enemy of the Empath

ADDITIONAL WORKS
BY AUTHOR

The Sacramentum
Tarot/Oracle Cards

THERE IS NO TRUTH UNTIL
YOU DECIDE WHAT TRUTH IS

Grand Master
Dr. Delbert Blair

www.ingramcontent.com/pod-product-compliance
Lightning Source LLC
La Vergne TN
LVHW011402080426
835511LV00005B/383